Organic Hotels

Selected poems, and a story

by Matthew Abuelo

All material within these pages are the sole property of Matthew Abuelo and cannot be reproduced without his promotion. Doing so will lead to legal actions.

Copyright Year: © 2007

ISBN 978-0-6151-6898-2

for Vivian

"I'll die for your sins if you live for mine."
From the works of Jim Carroll, "Silent Money"

Index

Forward	7
Untitled	8
Photographs	9
Mass Transit	12
Untitled	13
Public Transportation	13
The Death of the Unknown Poet Van Gogh	14
Dead Sea Scrolls	15
Toxic Love	16
Blind Cave-Fish	16
Room 202	17
Variations of The Same Theme	18
Hairline Fractures	18
Untitled	20
Untitled	21
Tiny Earthquakes	22
Winter 2002	22
Lament for the Death of my Libido	23
Screams from the Island	24
Scattered Visions of the 21st Century	25
The New Prayer	29
Organic Hotels	30
Untitled	31
Untitled	31
Untitled	32
Cat Skin	34
Untitled	35
Cross Roads	36
Kingdom of Misfits	37
To Hunter S Thompson	39
Midnight Day Dream	40

Untitled	41
The Art of Writing	42
Song of the Abbots	43
8 ½	45
Two Angels	47
The Smile of the New Buddha	49
Untitled	51
Song of Silence	53
Talking To Mao	54
The Fall of the Colossus	54
Untitled	55
The Art of Fear	56
Time Piece	56
The Night Buffalo	58
The Dexter House	59
Cleansing The City	60
The Strange Garden	61
Untitled	62
Last Night of CBGBs	64
Visions Of The Future	64
Exit Zero	69

Forward

In the early 1980s, novelist and poet William S Burroughs stated that there was no movement in the United States either on the social or literary level. While this might be partly true, at least on the level of making a statement on a revolutionary scale or making any true evaluation about the current state of our culture, there does seem to be a movement within the world of poetry that suggests the art is becoming more of a hollow shell of itself. With a few exceptions, most of the newer, recognized poetry books read like Hallmark writers suddenly moved to take up "serious writing".

For the most part this second book resembles more of what I had envisioned for *Last American Roar* which was published in the summer of 2003. At the time, I was still looking for a voice that I could truly call my own which I accomplished later in LAR. My vision for this second book is to rediscover what the older artists already knew. That is, the aim should be outside the writer, governed by that that which is greater than themselves. This is my attempt at a new movement, one which goes back to the core of classical writing, to accomplish on the page what Degas set out to do on the canvas. The aim is to create something that lives on long after I'm gone. All artists are vessels whose purpose is to create art then fade away. That is the vision for Organic Hotels, to reach that peak.

Untitled

Where are the zones where we can hide from the perverse loins of strange creatures who peer at the naked city through the invisible eye of the camera? At the core of western culture is death fermenting,
turning the city
outside the suburbs into drunken sidewalk theater,
bar brawls and towers of greed where the new czars lust for the
black fruit of desert vines whose roots reach deep into the sands of Babylon
only to be consumed in the intestine of Old Glory
all to be sold on the TV by salesmen of images,
pimps with the souls of smiling vampires.
At the center of Long Island is superficial boredom,
(shallow waters of Long Island boredom where scavengers feed on decaying lines of severed connections like craw fish feeding on the remains of their fallen comrades,)
and wet dreams of neighbors with their skirts hiked up while their husbands are away in the desperate prisons of currency.
The muted streets
the creation of new religions
the creation of gods of the modern age
to entertain us
and who we can punish when our dreams run dry in the sterile existence of the suburbs
(all connections are severed like those of inmates in isolation chambers in a distant penitentiary,
making comrades with the spiders,
Sparrows,
and vessel-less voices that reverberate through the skull as is if they were being shot out from invisible transmitters that dissolve into burning green glow of tranquilizer dreams.)
or to propose when we want to destroy the stranger that we've grown tired of entertaining.
The Island is a screen
exhibiting cinema of desperation,
drama,
tragic comedy by nature, without desire at its end.

House wives on the latest anti-depressants
fascism in a bottle
death by prescription.
This is the canceled voice of art,
depression without an outlet and surprised in dormant zones of genius.
Diseased flesh at cancer clinics waiting for radiation treatment.
GE sludge washing up on the shores of the sound.
Let us leave this sad theater and find the tribes that welcome us.

Photographs

The photographs were clear
the smiling faces over a human pyramid,
the flesh structure of shame of a land that is older and wiser than your
hatred and horrible misunderstanding of the world around you;
the one you were taught was so evil but it's soul is more pure then your
anger at those you were taught to be seen in the black lens of apocalyptic
fear.
And Old Glory cries,
she cries at the shame you brought to her.
Her name is tattered and soiled by your moves
in the glowing Baghdad night.
She cries at her rotting image in holy Baghdad,
she cries at the red waters of the Euphrates.
She cries at the insect swarm of her children on a city in flames.
She cries at the ever expanding images of Abu Ghraib prison.
And you,
you kneel there grinning with a slave's grin as the stock market Molochs
feed,
they feed on the last remaining resource with green tongue empire
the black fruit that calls for no one
but is plucked by the hand of
shock and awe
shock and awe
shock and awe
shock and awe.
But those underneath will rise again.

They will rise from the desert sands,
they will raise from their soccer field graves of Fallujah,
they will rise from the rubble of Basrah,
they will rise with the glow of a young revolution.
And they will rise from the cradle of civilization
where science and mathematics were conceived
and art
and poetry were born.
They will rise on the horses of their ancestors and drag you under into the
Nuremberg pasts of hanging faces of those who came before you.
Those born in Auschwitz souls.
Listen to the winds
listen to the winds
as the whispers of their ancestors tell you of your fate,
the sign of you of your fate.
And your ancestors stand there smiling
you won't kill in their name any longer.
The Moloch of the city will no longer feed in their name
for the profit of another stock market gain
The lowest common denominator,
your ruler to measure the value of human worth.
But
Their ancestors are coming on the winds of an on coming storm there's
nothing you can do about
not with bombs,
depleted uranium blowing back in your face like a messenger
of the ages letting you know they are waiting for you,
to drag you down.
Storm clouds forming overhead
and there's nothing you can about it.
The clouds are starting to form the roads of the
12 horsemen.
They know you.
No need to run or hide
they'll peer through your window grinning at the failed attempt
as you crawl and beg on your belly.
The moment of your second great shame.
The eyes of the world are upon you.
The eyes of Fallujah are upon you.

                The eyes of Najaf are upon you.
            The eyes of Tripoli are upon you.
                        The eyes of Ramada are upon you.
            The eyes of Basra are upon you
                        The eyes of Moscow are upon you.
        The eyes of Ho Chi Min City are upon you.
            The eyes of Geneva are upon you.
                        The eyes of Bangkok are upon you.
            The eyes of Wounded Knee are upon you.
But the black fruit that enslaves your lust that expands in the throats of
                            babes,
                                women
                        men
            and elders of the first great civilization
                                who are so faceless to you
                    statistical loses,
                                collateral damage.
These people you can't erase only to recreate their stories in history books.
                    your book of lies.
The horns of Ramadan will blow again in celebration of your withdrawal
                and the new day brings true democracy.

Mass Transit

This is the last station,
        the end of the line.
All stadiums vacant.
Sound waves still reverberate from
        rodeos
ball games,
        rock n' roll
and the fanatic cheers of hollow vessels.
We have reached the end of one century only to be consumed by another,
    blood thirsty
        eyes of space and vacuum.
It's pressure leveling the cradle of thought
reversing the evolution of man as he/she barks in worship of the moon
digesting Babylon in all consumption of the nuclear towers.
    Listen Children,
those who we handed power over to have grown insane in the forests of
    currency
draping themselves in Old glory's blinding light of belief where America
    fights to sleep.
We must shed them like snake skin and toss them into the fires of revolution
    like virgin sacrifices,
        for the gods are not pleased.
And we should not be pleased with the work of fools.
And the earth, sick and grey in her chemical waste, is not pleased as her
    children wage war on her tender side.
The weapon of truth is quickly fading into the state of the
    news factory.
This is the invasion of the pituitary gland.
The voodoo winds bring the stench of the shit dogs that live in the teeth of
    false kings who rule with ceramic faces.
And Cereus shitting on the subterranean culture of New York,
    then plummets deep into the Hudson river
        among the tapestry of newspapers,

                                used condoms,
                   syringes,
                              and mobsters,
                                          dead and stiff.
        INS pulls him out and charges him with a felony.

Untitled

It is common knowledge that the costumes of wealth alter the senses
                to a point of white light,
    all performers become blind cave-fish only moving with the instinct
                    of privilege
        with their minds hiding the doors to vision
    with the stench of the rotten fruit of promise falling from their lips
      forming pools where tiny iridescent fish come to feed on the silent
                  release of desperation.

Public Transportation

        Riding public transportation is like being under a microscope
                    you're surrounded by parasites.
    And you don't know where the next one is coming from and you can't
                        expect its arrival.
                                    Before you know it,
                    She's talking your ear off.

The Death of the Unknown Poet Van Gogh

His name and words meant nothing to the city
but,
those who heard each line like an on-going tide
came to visions of the aborted Christ
a genius that was reposed.
The streets filled with tears,
women came with excitement.
But,
none of his books sold.
This is the price he had to pay for mocking death,
his genius falling through the cracks in the sidewalks.
Another Van Gogh goes unnoticed.
Like so many young artists before him who drowned in the mediocrity
around them.
But Van Gogh,
I know your genius.
I feel it in me ever day
It's furious and unforgiving flow
that will not save us
or the ear that you pierced with the straight razor.
The wheel is still turning for us but,
the gears are starting to lock.
You were not going to end it like him.
No.
Not with a gun or in the wheat fields that still grow to pay homage to his
blood.
The concrete was where the conception of your demons took place and it's
here that you still fill your pockets with the words that form lines in the eye
of time.
You were going to perform the final ritual,
Strange celebration.
And they were going to wonder how another Van Gogh receded into the
night,
unnoticed.

Dead Sea Scrolls

The albatross I have shot down will not keep in these stagnant waters where
parasites,
scum,
and women of need gather as a reminder of how fast your life can stop in the
suburban tombs.
Nor will I wait for your name to appear in the obituary column in the early
addition of Sunday's paper.
I know that you've spent a lifetime trying to perfect your death,
making it an art form.
Someplace to write your signature.
But the more you think in terms of lines
the higher you will rise,
until you reach the heights of a Mexican plateau.
And all lines become ledges that move closer together.
When you finally jump
like an actor from a fifth story window,
high on acid,
you will gain speed in your free fall until you hit concrete.
This is where you realize that you've always been grave-crawling,
never reaching the heights that you thought were possible.
And that face at the bottom is your reflection in the waters of the Dead Sea.
But your name is still alive,
fighting off all shadows of bullshit from the next joker.
But your name,
Merry,
sounds like God,
brings me to my knees in prayer that carries me to
shark-skin clarity.

Toxic Love

Love with the potency of strychnine.
It comes at you like a car crash,
Devolving it's onlookers who become human mosquitoes,
unable to turn their heads from the blood scene,
being drawn into a white or blue light.
If this is heaven,
as many would suggest,
then I want to find my comrades in hell and discard any notion that space
ends between the thighs.

Blind Cave-Fish

We're walking blind in the city tonight,
eyes blank,
stares vacant of thought.
We're unaware of the screams of dreams that go up in flames on the
Baghdad horizon,
the homes of ordinary men.
And compassion
always undefined is the first victim of a city bloodthirsty and
a smoking gun waits around each corner.

Room 202

It's obvious that she's been around for a while with her
decaying connections.
Her form is a testimony to her mother, who is cheating death in a Florida
hospital,
connected to wires and tubes,
pale and loveless like a hydraulic puppet from a 50's B movie,
seen only at 3 in the morning,
which now feeds on shadows in a museum that is just beyond her finger
tips.
She knows there are just so many ways you can change the definitions of
your own passing
making an art form out dying in fragments or jumping in with both feet into
the swarming lights of addiction.
Her junkie fingers caressing a pack of cigarettes and valium
The monkey came knocking a long time ago for a fee that goes beyond the
currency of flesh.
This is hunger on the cellular level,
thousands of tiny mouths waiting to feed on synthetic skin.
But,
there are times she still smiles in the face of what remains of her,
in defiance
as if dying and fucking were the same act.
The motions I have to admit are similar.
This is the price of living too long in a skin that sleeps to hide its terrestrial
form,
that reeks into the hallways of cheap buildings where flies gather in lust and
pay homage to her,
that is,
her canceled form behind the door
while the funeral fires grow bright in the voided night.
And pall-bearers flood the room with formaldehyde and I raise the flag to
half mast in the memory of her
now that she's gone.

Variations of The Same Theme

Why do we worship between the serpents jaws?
Is it to gain the acceptance of TV eyed strangers that howl
at the cheapest performances only to wear a killers cloak?
In our cranium prisons we sit in silence in the invisible theater of women,
eating the bitter fruit jealousy. This is the ancient tradition of man.
The grave yard games belong to others.
The game of youth is ours to defend. This I will do with the infinite vision
of a child right before he learns the art of fear and the vision wilts like sea
lilies in oil slicks.

Hairline Fractures

The only consistency is
the consistency of gravity.
The weight of its pull cropping angel wings,
misfits falling to the glowing city where everything we know,
is what we have stolen only to recreate in the image of the cancelled genius
of the treasures we sleep to hide.
Our only escape is sweat house visions and the metamorphosis of recreating
our form into anything else but this dying museum where the virus of
addiction feeds on all we have saved,
implanting herself into our spinal cords
opening the fluid like liquid flowers that line the steps of an ancient
French,
New Orleans,
hotel,
where pale thighed whores go to weep for something that never sleeps.
But
we must make a deal with the preying mantis,
swallowing her whole.
She consumes this infection which we wear like a medal of honor for
surviving the night instead of lying next to a wooden box with silver coins
in our eyes.

2

Misfits everywhere,
listen.
The poles are starting to reverse,
changing the flow of the tides that move inside,
turning hissing lunatics into saints that harvest their youth in the side of
chaotic dreams
where what we try to hide glows in depths far below where angels dare not
fly.
And each turn takes the terrifying form of
asylums,
el Diablo,
John Merrick robed,
then naked and deformed,
shivering in front of an audience of salivating surgeons with hard-ons for
sideshow flesh
obscure gods of leper colonies who wonder in infection and hallucinating
dreams,
the rotting landscape of disease.

3

With the right eyes you can see the strings of TV salesmen,
schizophrenic journalists
who look into the lens of the camera with a crustacean's eyes,
emotionless and void of thought.
The emotions here are false,
the cover of insect specialties and gimmicks.
All strings pulled by monsters who dwell in the strange swamps of currency,
making comrades with black marketers of
black petrol wars.
And with those eyes,
you can see the tides of time reverse until time itself stops,
the 7th horseman straddling his horse with a sardonic smile and we sit in
our rooms with phantom memories and write our last words of roads that
break in two,
all is lost,
all is lost,
all is lost.

Untitled

I'm sick of uncovering the tyranny of your flesh in the endless equations of chance.
This is the game of chance,
to hand your future over to strangers now or be forgotten at the top of the stairs looking into the far reaching depths,
seeing your reflection smiling sardonically
at you.
This is vertigo,
the fear of falling,
all senses altered,
the warm pleasure of vomiting rose petals from this latitude
in the hope that she returns like some vague royalty.
Enlightenment,
the animal that waits for us at the gates of suffering,
Pouncing on us with vicious intent as we realize all our true forms,
infinite.
Did you know that all our moves are temporary,
lovers that recede into the deepest recess of the mind,
the deserts of emotion.

Untitled

We've reached the limits of the city,
the architects of our elaborate plans,
creating the myths of the new gods now that we've reached the last
reminisce our youth
escaping the shore that sleeps to devour what we have saved.
Its savior will not bleed for you
but
will bleed you of all your true desires
leaving you limp no matter how many ways you try to get it up.
There is a new age rising
it's true that we must make a deal with the planets to keep from being
crushed by their gravity.
But this deal is high,
each atom of this solar system collapses,
creating flashes of white light,
deadly and radioactive,
under the weight of her touch
scattering all our true loves into fragile white pearls that shatter like a rotted
tooth bite.
And you can't solve the mystery of its coming or the origins of its desire.
This is where felons become saints,
their palms bleeding becoming the resurrection of Christ,
or glow with a corral reef green light and become the Buddha himself and
transcend time and space until time losses all form and dissolves all
meaning into our deep dog instinct for survival in this warm place where we
crash at night,
out from the shadows of heroes who can't live outside their skin of
contempt,
and in the morning we will enter the wild with the last droplets of our
dreams in our hair.

Tiny Earthquakes

A quick fact about earth quakes
Did you know they cause the earth to gyrate,
causing great tidal waves,
walls of water 55 feet high the papers said.
The last great one washed away brown peasants and gaudy Euro-flesh.
But here,
in no specified place,
I deal with a much greater force of nature.
I can't seem to escape the last vapors of your images tonight, Merry.
They stay with me like a well-trained monkey that never seems to leave my
side, even in times of chaos and disorder of a LA riot caused by a video tape
and 12 blind jurists.
I tried to cut it loose but,
it always has a way of finding its connections in gray membrane.
But my thighs still bleed from straddling this fence,
to call you one more time
or to sever all my connections.

Winter 2002

Winter 2002
First real winter in eight years.
Frozen dog breath from around the corner
The dog god
Holy figure of tribal savior who wears the head of the nocturnal hero
On the end of a chain.
The pulse of the city,
8 million stories of desperation
Each looking to be reborn in the concrete womb prisons.
Let's live on the pulse of the city like an electric Messiah.
Life on long Island,
Grave yard of experience remains,
Boredom consumed.
Bone dust of imagination.
Where are the burning riots we were promised?

Lament for the Death of my Libido

Lament for the death of libido,
Young wet cunts weeping in the summer night.
I dream of Christ,
Crucified in the shit-yards of Riker's
(the judge railroaded him on bum rap)
overlooking the dark soft and tender side of the wild wilderness
pitch black except for the distant lights of a vacant neon light motel,
the desk clerk jerking off to faded pictures of skeleton faced
models
I dream of you in front of the women's bathroom while snake charmers
tame your thighs with notes that beat against your smooth pale flesh.
Isotope jaws in the anal cavity of young catholic school boys
Waiting to feed on priestly jism.
TV cunts squeezing out the images of curdled milk flesh
Of street walkers who go down on bored suburban businessmen.
The air is filled with sound bites of,
Politics,
Death salesmen who preach for black petrol wars.
Hey man.
Who could get hard on in this atmosphere?
Just gave smoking weed,
dig?
Its been awhile since I've done it straight.
There's always a fear of Cumming to soon.
Lament for the death of my libido.
Thoughts of whores with hydraulic lifts on the heels of their shoes to
withstand the night that comes at 1000 miles an hour.
And I stand here in my apartment,
broke as usual and out of beer and weed.
Masturbation has become much too familiar and would make a better
stranger than say,
A heart that beats in empty space only to be engulfed into a lovers fist.

Screams from the Island

Long Island,
Silent museum of desperation,
Streets and sidewalks as soulless as concrete zombie flesh.
Like any other parasite it feeds.
It feeds on the lives of couples and children and actors who sleep alone.
In its place are desperation, Chinese whores, weed and excess of money and broken teeth.
Wall Street boys with faces in snow
Eskimo pale lips blue as a whale's ass.
Suicide letters washed away in midnight rain showers.
Pharmaceutical drugs washed down with wine and brandy or beer. And chased with hash.
Banks creep up on every corner like pale lunatics in Nyquil dreams,
And just as faceless.
The best I can hope for is having the weight of this boredom crush every word of this page,
Every line in this book
Into fine ash then planting it in this cancerside soil and hope black fruit grows,
Rotted out before the vine begins to flower.
Cops roll by like suburban vampires looking to rail road the next young-faced hood.
And I dream of you on West 86th street,
On my way every weekend,
In the subways listening to the next evicted cat give us the New York subway serenade.
Ladies and Gentlemen: "I'm homeless and if you can help me out…"
And he knows he will never make it to the Island,
Cause if he did,
They would club him and dump him off in Freeport,
or Hempstead,
or East Amityville,
or South Oaks.
His words will never penetrate the gated communities of Muttontown.
His fingers will never make it passed the security guards of Great Neck.
And he would never be remembered cause they would put up another bank
where he would have died and send his ghost up the river to Riker's Island.

But he's still in the subway with a look of defiance that says,
"I'm not dead yet mother fucker."
I love you so much Vivian some times I get nervous,
You know?

Scattered Visions of the 21st Century

The announcement,
"Ladies and gentlemen, I'm homeless and I don't use drugs. If you could help me out I could feed my children. I have three little girls and I have aids."
This is the New York subway serenade.
The game of sex
The dance of death
Their intent,
I have to admit are the same;
To reach the point of white light,
Beyond the furthest things
Or fall below the waterline.
Did you know that climax is the death of the game?
Look at what we've become,
Blind cave fish that scatter under the foot steps of Shaman or tyrants;
Who stagger in silence in costumes of wealth.
Their masks of ceremony,
The first,
The face of death,
Birth and back again
The other,
Nero of the modern city.
They move in dances of hysteria to reach the corral reef green light of vision
or fade into the red light of a city in flames.
Television,
Impudent box of images
Ball games
Salesmen of artifice
Sterile game show hosts with hungry grins for the modern day lobotomy

Prisons of boredom
Faceless tricksters flood the cerebral landscape with shit-whore flesh.
Do you remember your life without commercials
Running in the wilderness with a tribe of friends.
I prefer this forest to a highway of pale lunatics who chant into the gothic
garden and among the desert flowers where all words are worn and all tears
Fall into the sand of divine temperament.
As Malcolm said,
This is the time for martyrs.
When all television screens are shattered then we will reach our golden age
The end of time,
The end of the line.
And all false saints will be exposed and all true angels will be set free
beyond mans' remains and decree.
Did you know that the lust for life has faded,
The aborted fetus of genius in pools of afterbirth where even Jesus weeps
With his long judging finger.
Come on out Jesus!
We know you're in there.
Look at the century that you left us.
What madness is the mind of genius surrounded by a storm of naked
children as helpless as a cripple in a foreign landscape;
Who feed on the heels of rabid dogs who breath down the necks of babes?
This is the diseased year of our lord 2004
Where I've witnessed the tide of men fall beneath the waterline,
Into pools of fear of breathing
Like a Baghdad scholar under the watchful eye of the new Moloch
who drapes himself in old glory.
The horns of Ramadan blow in sorrowful celebration of mystical tale of the
fading cradle of history.
This is the fear of living in the west where death smiles in cool blue 'shroom
dreams
Where we fuck our primal ancestor in her dance of fire.
Invisible aides soldiers pillage African villages.
Africa screams tearing the fabric of time and century.
Broken winds race across the plains,
Great lion roar
Wildebeest male heat for the last cow
the first sex

Snakes copulate by the last water pool of spring.
This is survival in its most basic form,
Moving with insect quickness in the storm that ruffles the chiefs feather.
Let us leave our beds before the days early cry where we never learn how to
die right in this belly of the asylum we call home
and where mad men play their ancient games of risk with the blood of
young boys as the stakes.
But I want to spend one more in the city before we escape its wisdom
That dies on the outskirts of town,
To rediscover the forgotten gods of this land that still smiles
in the prayers of the Indian ceremony,
Peyote celebration.

2

What culture is our culture,
To let the next Van Gogh go unnoticed.
The culture of the streets is the culture of rage,
tattooed fingers moving across the equatorial lines to find the right blade
for a homicide.
the culture of fear,
suffering in ivory tower prisons.
In the suburbs,
everything is on surface
nothing swims or exists below.
Even hot flashes of aging house wives lack all depth,
As they cook up their true desires with black coffee to dead-eyed husbands.
The moves of the suburbs become the march of sleep where we dream in
organic motels
where youth dances with phallic senses.
on the stage models deconstruct their forms as they move down
runways
with bird-like beauty.
This is the suffering of the black comedy,
to spend the body in plastic hallow of belief
with fame at its end.
Flashes go off in sparks of white light.
The camera watches all-knowing god
never satisfied until all images are consumed and all youth collapses.

But fame has a price,
a proposition with the monkey who always comes to collect with
ancient hands that will never be severed no matter what the myths say.
And no amount of pills delay his arrival.
All debt must be repaid with an interest that grows as time passes into
concrete and latent flesh which
only enhances his anticipation.
Before you know it you're
performing the New York subway serenade
"Ladies and gentlemen I am homeless...."
Listen children,
loot the stranger with jewels in his eyes that has come to our house,
Mexican whore house,
a guest that doesn't know when to leave,
like chaos around a rifle with a rose in its
barrel.
Look at the century that waits for us each morning
with the clarity of new born
and with death at its center.

The New Prayer

I've grown weary of the old mouth biting at my ankles.
Oh how I'd love to crush her skull under the heel of my shoe and watch the
dust blow away in tornado-like rhythms
in the soft,
gentle breeze.
I have no more use for dead-eyed idols of decaying wisdom.
What time is it in your pale skin
which drapes over your skull and bone like a costume addiction.
Must we be slaves to the penitentiaries of this rotting and dead culture with
its vast bone yards where our enemies dance in costumes of death,
wedding dress of bone dust,
lock-jawed tyrant?
This is their ritual,
the long judging finger of an ancient spinster.
this is the steel prison of the American mind,
trapping young thoughts,
starved,
mad,
screaming and beaten boy the tongue of the sheriff,
gun on hip,
of this institution.
Basra angels dance in the strange rituals of eternal night in their charred
flesh.
American courts grow rabid with the needle,
Injecting us with a counterfeit leader,
Puppet fool of a dying kingdom.
Oh God give us a new land,
A new garden where we can travel and harvest our youth;
To build great monuments to celebrate our escaping this insane ritual of
currency
Soft sanctuary with the potential of infamy.

Organic Hotels

What time is it behind your eyes
                        now that she's gone?
Each of her attempts were distinct in their feel
                        Like stones pressed deep into our palms
          Leaving red marks along each line.
Blood washing over the stones before we threw each one back into the
                    water
In our pale attempts to return part of ourselves back to the sea.
      There are no more charms on the floor of the gypsy cab
                            No more deals to be made
             The price is far too high,
No more prayers in the rooms of the organic motels where all connections
      are severed under the blade of transient wisdom.
Fruit flies moving in and out of focus in the early morning sun light,
          The smell of chlorine still in your hair,
              and on your lips.
      The stench of pink remains of the nights' excess,
                       this is bitterness and rage taken form
before we swallow ourselves whole with midnight day-dreams of when we
              fucked in Long Island hotels,
             On my birthday and wrote poems of
             and odes to our death.
                 Wake up!
      The city is hungry again and on the hunt.
         Did you know the road is calling us back?

Untitled

Why must we conspire with the tyranny of her moves as we die awake
Into this living museum where tiny coups over throw the royalties of night.
But we are free form her disguise as host,
lover,
carnival daughter who leaves street culture fools in hair shirt frenzy.
she walks under the bright lights of her big top lies,
like dogs that sleep in her dreams, at the mouth of sanity.
And it in these dreams where I cannot breath
under the stars whose constellations tell the story of those dreamers lying in
the grave yards of pride,
Castrated by her smile.
this act is not unlike a straight blade used in a homicide.
Forget the news
Our end comes on the hooves of animals as they race from the
forests as they hear her foot steps pass like a whore that taste the theater
lights when she laughs.

Untitled

The American politicians at best are mounds of latent flesh;
A product that the people of the western lands neither need nor desire but,
like any consuming nation, the act of purchasing is an insect-like specialty.
It takes no thought and the vessel must conduct all actions as part of its
nature. And who sells these products, diseased in their form? The major
corporate slave syndicates, with their soulless green masks of wealth. They
feed on the carnivorous buffet of skid row. But it doesn't take long be for
their terrestrial form is exposed,
thick jelly oozing from every orifice of their
bodies,
forming pools of rotten ectoplasm sludge. They are in perpetual heat (the
sexual desire of a eunuch) at the thought of war,
feeding one million Iraqi bodies to the sinister belly of old glory.
The tool of this modern day lobotomy is the television,
The assembly belt machine of fantastic news, devolving the modern male.

And brother it's working. For the modern man,
The bombardment of exhausted sport,
Violence,
desolate sex, mindless rants of born-again Christians and schizophrenic
journalists giving the Bronx cheer for the dissolving blue light of the
constitution,
condemning freedom of the free lands. Only the body is human;
the mind,
soul, behavior and culture are simian.
In the streets
angelic protestors with the innocent hearts of cave children who see the sun
for the first time,
smile with defiance,
blue uniform storm troopers crush all dissent with sexless heat in the heart
of the news factory.
God we need a revolution.

Untitled

The fruit of chance is ripe on the vine
But its' skin is unusually thin,
Exploding in the hands of those who fall into reason.
Did you know that we've moved from the bodies of young architects of our
realities invention,
Holy perception of youth,
The innocents of cave children who see the sun for the first time
Potential to reach great heights while attempting to avoid being devoured by
our mother's neurotic moves and keeping one step ahead of her blade that
she fashioned to castrate us.
The self image of being young in
wet flesh is as brittle as pressed dragonfly wings
moving into the bodies of servants who show obedience to sexless desire of
currency.
The game of currency to soul
has one basic rule,
the more you gain the more you loose.
The game of wisdom to youth has a similar law,

the more you gain the more death smiles in your bedroom window.
Insanity is an undercurrent,
bottomless ocean with warm inviting tides.
Suicide letters on two-way mirrors
empty antidepressant bottles on her bedroom floor.
Like any domestic animal,
youth are wild with potential
eyes burning with grey matter desire to play the game
with sex at its center
only to be broken
domesticated and locked in cubicles
eyes fade into lifeless jewels.
Old dogs crawl deep into the wilderness to die,
eyes diluted
Tail between their legs with paralyzing fear of the inevitable.
Old New Yorkers crawl shamelessly to Florida and buy immaculately sterile
death condos,
warehouses, really
where morphine hazes fade to black.
If all the residents of Miami cemeteries stood up all at once
Florida would have one hell of a population problem.

Cat Skin

He came from across the fields,
The animal of the Pharaohs,
The gods in form
animal of Christ with Lucifer laughing in his eyes.
Tiny beads of blood around his mouth from the nights excess
The menstruation of *le petit mort*
red pools of aborted current
it was a bird
he found in diseased pools of the run-off from the storm two days ago.
He found his body in Battery Park but,
his sanity was still in the opium fields of Vietnam
where he died,
and he died today
and he'll die tomorrow
and he'll die a little next year.
And he'll die in the news factory that works overtime,
emanating static that drowns out the screams of young revolutionary hearts.
And he'll die in dreams of the Mai Lai massacre.
And he's dying with unknown and unspeakable parasites that incubate in his
cranium,
grow
lay their eggs, then die.
And he knows that you can't be king in this place when the flowers at your
feet are newspaper
clippings.
Obituary columns, of course
of all the people you know.
And it's hard to set the
stage when there are no more roles to play.
There no more day and night
no and night and day.
Did you know our
days are numbered?
And he looked into the New York moon with a sardonic smile in statistical

visions of a city in crisis.

Untitled

I dream and think in terms of electric chairs,
Shock treatment,
Live wires that burn along the concrete,
Madness screaming.
This is how you know that you're alive,
Electricity flowing through the membrane,
Bringing you back to yourself,
The first self.
Buddha smiling in black hash fields.
The dog stands at the head of the stairs and barks in primal form.
He knows it like tracers that move through the cerebral tides of this
gathering;
He gives me a look as if to say,
Get your ass out of bed and let's go.
There is life to be lead.
Don't you know the bomb is going to drop any day now?
The television is the cerebral grave yard.
Dreams that flow like current that pass though the membranes of the reality
of false kings,
Puppet fools in insane towers of currency smiling with rotting desire
Over the dead frontier where Basra angels gather in their charred flesh with
white pearls between their thighs.
Come on we're leaving this decaying penitentiary of the Island where
infancy dies in the warm and bleeding womb of the dawn
And bring your gun we're going to find the thief of all our true loves,
With her brilliance.
But watch out for her smile,
Or your rage will vanish into a hard-on.

Cross Roads

African blues guitar being played on a southern crossroads
without vessels.
A nun stands on one corner with her bible
a whore stands on the other with her sins in her back pocket,
The strange figure she calls father waiting for her at home with a joint and a
hard-on
watching black and white screens of war on the television from
the pawn shop.
Tears of angels in flames falling from the sky forming fishless rivers with
acid rain death.
Apple orchards can be seen in the distance.
The fruit rots right before they fall.
Their trees form the signs of the gray and sorrowful land with her ripped
womb prisons,
gentle surrender.
If you listen close enough,
You can hear the vesselless voices with transmitter whispers,
"There's a storm coming and there's nothing you can do about it.

Kingdom of Misfits

A night in the city, a circus of lights,
bells and
whistles, Time Square is a fuckin' pin ball machine in a mad arcade
with naked capitalism at its center,
an assault on
the senses.

For those of you who
want to visit the great city, stay the hell out of
Time Square. Visit the village. A Ghost Town of
artists. Or at the very least stay the night at
the Chelsea. Open your cells to the genius of the
great heroes at the nerve center of art. Hunt for culture not
some damn shortcut to
dissolving the human form.
Where are the great minds that roamed on the fringe,
wild,
crazed,
snarling,
Lucifer laughing in their eyes
their childhoods dripping from their lips onto cold pavement?
If you want to handle the scene of Time Square,
you must rewire your circuits,
avoid the great onslaught of the neon tapestry of sound,
images and endless advertisements,
the mind reverberating like screeches of banshees in your window during
an acid frenzy.
The stares of six hundred foot posters smiling down as all-knowing Gods.
Time Square is a beast reincarnated from the wild eyed blue flame of the
1980s.
This is the nerve center of naked capitalism,
the perfect place to bury yourself in lights.
A great alter of a religion with an energy source
antique Buddha's as an excuse of holding some
factory holiness.

The mystics that kept the tide of music flowing through the veins of
emotional refugees and the subway stations
Before each note was crushed under the weight of a dream that came out of
the industrial age only to go terribly wrong
being put up for sale on stock exchange floors
from ticker tape continuum to computer down fall.
The pin ball machine has grown hungry,
vicious,
savage like a predator in Germanic black forests.
The horrid wave of currency flooded the roach hotels washing away the
vagabonds,
vagrants,
squatters and pale lunatics under the water line,
sterilizing Needle Park.
The facial features of the city pulled under by the oceans' undertow.
Every city,
every town,
every village
is built on the remains of artists
whose ghosts wonder just out of the reach of
Riker's or
South Oaks or,
Sing Sing or
Auschwitz
The Wall Street boys invading the kingdom of misfits.

To Hunter S Thompson

Did the guards of this life stop you at the gates,
asking for your passport whose insignia was burned into surrealistic snake
skin leather by your devils of adrenacrome hallucinations,
who danced in Las Vegas hotels,
with tits on their backs. I know you're laughing with the great Brown
Buffalo again
(he ran with the roach people)
beyond the reach of Raoul Duke.
This place was never big enough for the both of you.
You said one of you had to go.
It's a good thing you were always dead on,
Never missed,
this time was no exception.
Did the tide of a generation pull you under,
With LSD madness at it's center where the dance of revolution and
innocence faded?
This is perhaps the high water mark to the west.
But drugs on the sleeve in the bathroom can't explain your great escape;
No great shark
or the turning of the tide,
the death of the heart of America.
The dream that came out of the industrial age dissipated into the cleft of the
mind and you will be there smiling with the great Brown Buffalo
or watching another football game with Nixon.

Midnight Day Dream

Under the pale light of the New York moon,
With street cars and vagabonds who cast themselves to the
Shadows,
I had a dream of grand buildings whose lobbies have felt
The Chelsea mercy of what time has forgotten.
On each floor were tiny sanctuaries where artists,
misfits,
and the cities refugees escape
the streets that show open nosebleed contempt for the human form,
to rest their bodies that were beaten and worn;
engage in conversations that we will never know or understand.
The lights of genius glowing bright.
But the dream changed.
In basements across America sat slumlords with used car salesmen souls,
with the heart of the cities clinched in their teeth,
deconstructing the facial feathers of those cities with the stroke of a
pen.
Here,
they flush out the weak and wipeout the endangered.
"Aren't you patriotic? This is naked capitalism. This is how the system works. For those who oppose us, send them to the fuckin' camps. If you want to go to heaven you must reach for a gun and take dead aim at those who steal the scraps from our tables in the form of social programs."
I awoke in a cold sweat,
praying that this was just a nightmare backwash,
the mind giving form to the terrors of a past life,
being raped in opium fields of Persia or Mesopotamia.
After unclenching my jaw I fell back to sleep,
slipping back into the same dream which changed yet again,
turning beautiful
wild spirits of times past.
When Tyranny's rejects came to release their dogs
the misfits,
artists
and refugees rose in defiance.

They raised their fists towards the sun with one foot in the grave.
They shouted words,
lines that had escaped their lips when they wore a younger skin
Hell no we won't go!
Hell no we won't go!
Hell no we won't go!
Hell no we won't go!
Hell no we won't go!
I just had to smile,
Victory was at hand.

Untitled

The secret angelic fingers are mixing the spinal fluid.
The boy who hunts for love in his sideshow flesh that he wears with
Magical real horrors
is the loneliest among us.
Plumes of white smoke hang over his
head
With the reflections of addiction trapped in his smile.
2
What blue flame haze have you cast yourself into
Sitting in roach hotels like a New York
messiah
With the most arrogant of need to sacrifice yourself to feminine black
veil desires and high heel shoe manipulation of the senses.

The Art of Writing

In art
the skull becomes a bleached cave where words and images become blind
cave-fish that swim with instinct in currents of electrical storms and
chemical embrace.
The eyes are crude spectators,
Voyeurs to this naked war of survival and dead currency.
The tongue is the extension of the genitals ferocious in its pursuit,
long angelic fingers of Petite De Morgue caress the synapses,
white explosion,
hard-ons and rapidly moving thighs.
Savage feminine fingers engulf the heart that beats in empty space.
Cool currents moving in waves though space and time until time itself stops
and all gears lock
and we learn to loose,
well.
Don't tell me of writers block.
Here we are God,
Saints whose followers are lost in wilderness,
praying silently to drink,
to fuck,
to dance frantically in the skin of leather-clad angels,
to serve no one,
We are archangels whose wings are words,
phrases and temples
And where we make our comrades in hell.
Here we are niggers of the layman's noose,
with eternity at our finger tips.
We put our pen to the paper like the steel of a blade to the throat to an all-
too-familiar stranger.

Song of the Abbots

The abbots of milk flesh still wonder among these roach hotels
Screaming
"What we are today you will be tomorrow
Tasting the fire of being forgotten. And we forgot
we forgot the flames of rage spreads as quickly as the silent wings of malaria."
Yellowed eyes of disease watch the crooked knife theater of digesting the features of the city
the Bottom Line dissolving into droplets of dreams in the hair of those who can still smile in the universities.
But tonight the abbots throw themselves to Blake's burning tiger,
Casting themselves to great jaws whose teeth reach depths where even the most militant angels dare not fly.
Screams permeate the shit-yards of the tombs.
The milk of your suffering has curdled but you drink from tainted glasses
with
grinder-monkey obedience
As if it was holier than yourself.
And we watch from the New York skyline among the antennas,
Spectators of the radio waves
with angelic eyes that see to the end of night.
Watching them (the abbots) being torn to shreds.
We are the new abbots walking hunched over from the weight of the city.
Huddled with blue prints of concert halls where we celebrate the voices of the children of the city
Who are just beyond the wanting jaws of conmen with offices at the universities and who hide behind masks of culture. Saints burn with the arrows of the Residents Committee who sat by in silence as affordable housing was being purged.
These are our cathedrals
where we dance with black leather-clad angels.
Women on the dance floor with mysterious smiles that break through the fabric of time and all nerves become wires that connect us to the end of the line,
the final station of rats,

suicidal remains and useless schedules.
And we sit under clocks with burning hands smoking with glowing hours;
books,
Lines
Phrases like,
"Love thy brother."
"Do not follow me but, seek what I once sought."
And watch out for the lunar tide that alters the oceans inside
Turning ordinary minds into glow lunatics.
The city is a stage of lunatics whose suffering is an umbilical cord to the fall
of the towers of currency.
"3000"
dead cried the headlines.
But who cries for Babylon in flames.

8 ½

If it is true as Fellini's priest would suggest
that everything outside the kingdom of God belongs to the devil
then all highways are avenues of slaves
chains around thighs,
ankles,
heart and mind.
We are all slaves to the gentiles with our sweet surrender
to pale flesh.
Sex in cheap motels and roach hotels of New York city.
America is an asylum where madness is accepted at its capital.

The Carnival Barker
"Ladies and Gentlemen: come all and witness the human condition
Spectral existence of burning comrades whose genius spirals into super
novas where hesitant fingers do not pass.
The cranium becomes a dry clinic,
An ash can for burned out connections.
Paralyses sets in with the impending fear of dying before I escape Long
Island.
The traps.
The perverted old doorman who smiles sardonically signifying an overly
friendly stranger with bad intention or a pale lunatic whose mind spirals
into oceans below the eye of wine,
synapses flooded,
electrical storms in the cerebral landscape of the on-going movie
in the fragmented theater of shapeless plots and whose scripts derive from
television sets,
newspapers
and prescription bottles that lay empty on filthy floors.
visions of drifting to the seas through the flames of a Viking funeral,
great Nordic horns cry through the mists of Puget Sound.
This is where the constellations take on different meanings.
The eye becomes a witness to March
the cruelest month.

This is when I was born,
the joke the gods played on me.
It's also the birthday of Albert Einstein so for years I celebrated this date.
But,
vicious irony,
This was the month of war which came in deadly form over Baghdad,
rain that explodes in the synapse.
The film of the on-going movie skips.
I don't celebrate my birthday much anymore,
April is open.

Two Angels

Paul Wellstone and Lenny don't live here anymore.
Check the room down the hall where we sit as spectators watching our lives
split in two.
You don't have to choose sides.
One moving through secret gardens of the glowing hours where the young
lie naked with smiles of possibilities,
Blowing plumes of smoke that form around the rail ways;
Exposing their genitals to the serpents of the act of loosing well
I saw the photos of the night you were gone,
naked
the needle still in the mainline,
Walden dissolving into the vein.
The line was served from its connection in the bathroom,
with the furious winds of price or chance.
Passion taken form
The burning snake that turns back on itself.
This was the baptism of a Jew in death
strange saint of the wasteland of trials and clubs of canceled voices.
Comedy is the most dangerous game,
Staying just out of the reach of the creeping fingers of the commission.
The senses expanding beyond control roaring while feeling the sting of the
prophets curse,
To stand before the lifeless sea of crustacean eyes which don't match the
laughter of mouths in disconnected cinematography.
Even the blue flame sanctuary of opium can't dissolve the images of a
country that turned back on itself.
This is the crime of the ongoing movie of dead actors and the scripts that
have given form to the Manhattan Project with blue flame vision of sterile
landscapes.
With the game of risk at its center.
The horrors of feeling the pleasures of the loins to the heart to the bottle to
the eye which acts as a witness to a vicious world in a feeding frenzy.
Laughter is that which combines all minds to one mind peeling back the
curtains exposing the last hints of drug ghosts who remain just out of focus
Like wax mannequins in a sex museum in under-developed film.
This is the politics of laughter,

The art to feel the embrace of wanting flesh or
To be shit out in crude Moloch consumption in operations as enemy of the state.

And you,
Wellstone
Was the debt to the devils of politics own flesh over due,
Where the smooth hand of negotiations could not pass.
Your idol jaw in the winter ether dissolves into lunatic time of politics,
The game of risk with insect simplicity.
The laws of politics
When you lie,
lie big
When you steal,
steal big.
No sense drowning in shallow waters,
back room deals,
writing and rewriting the scripts with Dada Dada confusion.
The film of the ongoing movie became brittle as pressed butterfly wings,
and snapped.
Winter snow,
grey night pays homage to the angle whose wings shattered in stained glass fashion
as the mind turned back on itself in blue silence.
The game of power becomes muted reason
Pale attempts in insect instinct.
But the silent fingers of death's blue flame has cast you to
savage shores of Babylon where iridescent murders
making ancient deals in back rooms
I know the fruit of your canceled voice still rots on the vines in the garden of the Pax-God whose control comes in the form of bank notes and virtual transactions.
But I wonder what line to take to reach you at the final station.

The Smile of the New Buddha

When humanity dies it is called the modern age.
When thought dies each mindless ritual becomes culture.
When Christ died his followers formed his death into the shape of a bullet
that dug deeper and deeper into the heart stems of the innocent.
And there all currents stopped and the modern circle of hell took form.
At 18 years of age hitchhiked across the American landscape
absorbing the holy satorie of being alive.
At 27 he died in the seas of 1000 tiny deaths in Paris that collapsed
in unequal parts.
At 31 he absorbed himself into a career.
Here true desires fades.
Money conquers soul.
Square lives kill belief.
The modern man becomes his own best domesticated animal.

2

We came from across the seas.
Our captain fell in love and fell onto these golden shores.
He now lies rotting in the formless night.
His cheek pressed and bleeding against tiled docks that lead to the peak of vision
peyote
hook in nipples,
connected to rope and tree
the farther you lean back,
the deeper you reach into timeless and formless space until you hit into nothing and all are healed.
Travel: escaping the death of the modern suburbs and reaching the idea the perimeters fade best in space-less infamy of the cerebral cortex.
Yoga
meditation: making yourself infinitely small and running with the ants in bliss and making comrades with the worms or becoming as large as the river until you become the river itself.
and your flow brings you to the forests of Buddha or the doors of the mad light that leads you to two paths.
One making you a lover.
One making you a killer.

New Orleans

In boredom the den of swine reverberates
with the squeals of orgasm from the Northern troughs
among the garbage heaps as the city of music created
by the hands of men returns to the sea.
What mind dissolves the music turning musicians into
enemies of the state?
There is an old bitch who lives on the perimeter,
moving her wet
long judging finger across the coast
first in the warm onslaught of concepts then later in
the angry winds of the cold womb tide.
Chemical fingers from the shit yards caress each note of blues,
jazz,
and tin pan alley rhythms,
pulling the southern heart below the waterline.

Untitled

I found this fork in the road that makes its connection in the synapse
where we must redefine ourselves in this dying museum
and where our anxieties hide in the strange rain of sleep.
When darkness dies all diaries must be rewritten.
There are no more drugs to keep this skin tight
all gypsy cabs have reached their final destination and all trains
have made it to the devil's station where Walt Whitman's vision of America
dies in unequal parts.
The factory doors have been closed with Andy Warhol's big sleep.
The wound of the bullet still runs deep in the flesh of art.
Do you still feel Valerie's fragmented breath on your tender
side?
The scars of the operation took years to run their course and you faded
into the continued images of a dream and edited frames of the on-going
movie.
The strange rain has drowned the New York voice as the city turns back on
itself.

The blue flame burns in the eyes of the Dexter house
where misfits smile with angelic fingers at the heart stem.
And I
looked for the Buddha on the Island.
For $75 you get a massage.
For $100 more she'll get you off.
But you don't have to sink so low to make connections in lonely women's
eyes or
to steal all the true idols between their thighs.
This is where the animal of instinct goes horribly wrong and we learn the art
of losing
well
and being forgotten.
The moment of clarity reveals herself with loving embrace 20,000 leagues
under the cross.
Down here
where the magical reality fades
there's no butterflies circling our feet.
There are no more miracles to buy with the jewels in our eyes.
The wires of voodoo vibrates as the ghosts of the tenements recedes
into the lights of the great pinball machine.
When the finger of clarity penetrates gray membrane
that tears then recedes where the lights never touch
then we know we're not holy
only forgotten.
This dance is over
with pornography on our tongues,
the obscenity of the eye.
The moves were too smooth,
there was nothing left to create in gray skin.
And like a Zulu warrior we let out a great battle
cry that tore the fabric of time and we fucked the night away.
Now the real dance begins,
to reinvent ourselves or to cast the theater in flames.

Song of Silence

The flesh recedes into the synapse whose current flowers into mad genius
with a silent touch
while wild orphans dance in tenements whose rooms are absent of
electricity.
The ghosts of the tenements sing the song of silence which expands in the
eardrums of gray New York and still can be heard above the hum of the
great pin-ball machine of Times Square
then dies in rotting wisdom teeth
the organic museums of words.
The eye is the witness to visions that do not matter.
When the nervous nights roll in then we'll know that the miracles and songs
of street profits merge with notes,
reverb,
and amp's static
then recedes into the cleft of the mind.
Fear becomes the new energy source in the politics of words and images.
And the specters of all generations vanish into the eye of the storm
With their young revolutionary hearts
And our lungs burn as we breath in the winter winds of their passing
The devil smiles on this strange highway.

Talking To Mao

Mao once said that to organize one must swim in a sea of people.
I say to travel in the Bronx one must swim in a sea of human wreckage,
where the streets rise up and whip you on the thighs.
What still lives in the trough turns skin fatal as it tries to break through
dreams that curdle like ancient milk to escape the house of swine
and midnight street lights
to find the cure that
vanishes into the rose garden that lines the temples of
another wisdom.
But the highway of sleep is never kind
you understand.
The devil's storm is always over the horizon running the synapse on over
drive in the desert of potential.
The city consumes the wild orphans of the tenements that lack all electricity.
Oscar Acosta turned a blind eye to these roach people that scatter under the
shadows of glowing factories that consume what remains.
When silence reverberates in the skull then is digested into the white noise
of fire fights on the angry streets
then we know that we've reached the gates of burning riots
that cleanse the western dynasty.

The Fall of the Colossus
(For Hugh)

Sooner or later the house will open to us all with embrace.
The dogs will lay at our feet in obedience
and welcome us.
And when the hand of eternal night washes over us in the bath
Of the great ether
The tides will roar in our ears to remind us that we were alive
and this heart that beats in empty space is in fact an orchid whose touch
leaves us confused and desperate like a pack of dumb beasts
the party will go on in some strange way.

Untitled

This is no place for hallucinogens
With flocks of peyote birds (in their green glow like effigies of saints
that wander between the lines of the grid,)
flying over the ocean of sterile dreams projected in endless advertisements
on 20 foot billboards of generic debutantes with lobotomy smiles.
We have been reduced to a pack of dumb beasts
in this wilderness of desperation and confusion
how couldn't we?
With the Charnel house waiting always around the corner.
The orphans among us wonder with blank eyes
wielding hammers on public buses
looking to smash in the skulls of their comrades.
Their anger burns far deeper than the crooked beak of meaning could ever
penetrate.

2

Put a robe on swine and put them on the supreme court
and feed them the remains of what was holy.
Abbie is crying in the great ether as the heart of Nixon is
pissing on the Ayn Rand backwash of politics.
Where are the burning riots we were promised?

The Art of Fear

What are these tides that beat against our thighs
Taking the form of ghostly fingers that never feel
but
consume
leaving the circles of fear burned into flesh?
They turn men into quivering children among a pack of dumb beasts.
Peyote night song take me home where the spirits die in equal
parts
And the post petit mort truth is the fire that never dies on the tongue of the
great snake.
Why does the mind turn back on itself like that snake
who swallows its own tail.
This is the hair shirt garment factory where the voice is canceled
and the skin fades.
Our sins fall to the floor.
The art is everything.
The vessel is irrelevant.

Time Piece

When the mind tears
Vision becomes a point white light that pulsates like a severed lizard's
tail.
The voice falls into squeals as the trough fills and the heart of desperation
becomes the fire that never dies.
Don't let the words be picked off the bone by scavengers that
fly high over the sky line looking for young artists to devour.
Shitting them over the city
over battery park
Down into the cracks of Christ's face which still weeps in the Cloisters,
Releasing their minds into the tombs where young beasts learn to feed

and we scratch at all locked doors to find the right key to escape into the
waters of sleep.
But
does Babylon still burn under your skin.
When the beast is satisfied then desire turns to fear that comes in with the
sewage of insomnia.

The canceled eyes become messengers that do no matter.
But
this is how we measure our time
following random women throughout the city like predators who
sleep in the dance of the game
always keeping our distance until the pursuit fades into each
century.

The Night Buffalo

The undercurrent of need comes in with a dull pain,
vague
like the earliest stages of a toothache.
Tongues whip against our thighs in blackened rooms where
wild orphans worship at the heels of women.
The need for money keeps us awake in New York SRO's
and brings the insomnia that comes on the heels of the night buffalo whose
hooves shake our days and rattle the skull.
Smooth arms become silk prisons where even sperm soldiers realize their
end.
Wisdom teeth continue their roles as the organic hotels of the obscenity of
words.
Do the strings to your heart stem grow thin as you drift into empty space?
Everything you spit in bitterness comes back at you twice as hard.
Even Salieri's notes grow mute with the defeat of time.
I know that you fall in love with these strange ceremonies
of death
birth
and back again.
This is when you realize that the skills that you have trusted all along
turn back on you.
And what you turn over is everything that you have borrowed.
This is where the gravity of fortune shifts
the poles reverse
turning the waters of fate into the sewage that washes in with the tides as
we play the burning violins in the symphony of hell.

The Dexter House

The Dexter House is a pauper's grave where the dead still dream of eternity
that shatters into cosmic silk which moves rapidly like an anemone that
captures the energy of 86th street
From the sex shops to the coffee houses and apartments where the worst of
human filth builds, (political pay-offs where the thieves come to collect.)
Here,
the only borders that matter are borders inside.
Those who make a habit of crossing each one avoids the horrors of reason.
Instinct becomes paramount in surviving this twisted circus.
The 16th floor is a dog show of rabid K9s that tear each other to shreds in a
strange flesh.
All chains have been broken and restraints have been severed
It's a savage orgy of dumb beasts.
Don't mention blood around them,
You'll only excite 'em.
Brazilians cower in dark corners in roach-skin suits
avoiding the savage Jew and southern carnival barkers that hunt for angels
in curdled milk flesh.
The jackals are sniffing around the door again.
Here the queer boys move in maddening fury with broken necks
like chickens in dead farms.
In the eyes of management the last reel of the on-going movie snaps
forming the graveyards of Ramadan angels.
If management survives,
that means something much greater has died.
Artists fashion their keys to find the right locks in the need of escape.
My habit becomes a ritual to be performed when I awake in room 411
at 12 in the afternoon,
after a Nyquil binge.

Cleansing The City

The city has turned back on itself
while its energy has become clumsy like an old Turk with a knife in his teeth.
This is where the heart becomes extinct
to be raised high into the twisted cathedral like a holy ode
to the truly strange.
Here saints wonder with newspapers on their feet and blue flame desires that
burn in their palms.
At the end of each night symphonies of burning
violins consume us in music of soulless notes and saturates the air.
The ghosts of the tenements and burned out galleries have grown mute
and have been cast into their own trail of tears.
For this new skin to exist the molting process has become violent.
A new metabolism is essential to break down the noise of the great machine.
The snake has died and Moloch has truly cashed in.
The ticket has finally exploded
And the show has gone terribly wrong.
When the burning machinery of the city no longer has a name
And the swine who own the SROs are sent to the killing floor
The beasts who stumble in the parade of the doomed lie obedient and beaten
and the cages of the tombs lie empty
then the only borders that matter are the borders inside.

The Strange Garden
(For Bill)

Some seeds fall into the strange garden.
Not all seeds will grow into orchids that blossom in the pale moonlight.
many will form hemlock served at the suppers of doomed kings
and those that don't
grow out
grow down.
There are those that become weeds that consume those of us that
were born of wine.
The bitterness that you have planted has grown deeper
and larger than the sum of its parts
with its vines tightening around your heart stem.
From this soil,
these weeds bear bitter fruit of losing with no strings attached.
What remains as your head lies in this furrow ground are dreams that
flower and smile sardonically.
These dreams have thorns that cut deeper than the roots tightening around
what lies below.

Untitled

The Dexter House
is the kingdom of the doomed
with tenants like Degas paintings come to life.
Down and out French women in darkened bars
with connections severed and burned out long ago.
Here the swine walk with canes and crawl at the feet of desk clerks with the
souls of cockroaches.
This is the end of the road
where the soul is naked.
In our accents of tastes,
lies our need to feast on something greater
art
the skin that recoils with the touch of genius
so we can perhaps escape this backwash and polluted pool of self
indulgence
where we become a parade of cripples.
That which quickens
the skull rattles with the thunder of tiny civil wars
between tenants who throw their ghosts to winds of uncertain futures.
This is where the mind devolves
making us all a pack of dumb beasts.
The landlord's jackals sniff at our door again wrapped in Jew and Southern
skin,
Then waits in the shadows cast by the storms in fright filled dreams.
The rabid dog show has become fierce on the 16th floor.
Tear down the elevators,
Let them tear each other to shreds in their aromatic lust.
Here on the forth floor we can hear Latin jazz through the air vents
a dog barks.
Artists hide deep within their rooms like military camps lost in the
wilderness.
Down below
under the totem of night
the ghost children still dance in the sacred fire we call upon

to cleanse our house.
The streets
are graveyards of culture.
Pop is the death of culture,
the last vapors of ancient notes.

2

Ode to the OTB the land of the roach people.

The sad museum whose rejected artifacts gather under plumes
of stale death,
cigarettes,
cheap liquor
and failure with no strings attached
The hangers-on remain behind in suits of door-to-door salesmen fit for a
pauper's grave.
That's the final bet Charlie,
Time to go.

Last Night of CBGBs

When will we stand on top of the great garbage heaps and look to the east
watching the seagulls vanish into the landscapes
as the storm finally breaks
so, perhaps we can win one more hour of silence.
The wave of frantic music played by leather-clad angels roll back below the waterline.
From up here we are still 20,000 leagues under the grey cross.
The last sounds from the violins of burning symphonies on stage has grown mute in the morning sunlight.

Visions Of The Future

We have reached the top of the garbage heap where we stand as witnesses to
the horizon of the on-coming tide,
the gland swells with excitement
but my lungs still burn from the white wall we tore down
the kingdom of misfits welcome us.
This is where we are reborn as cave children that see the sun for the first time.
The on-coming tide desires surrender and we surrender,
we surrender to the winter,
we surrender to the fall
we surrender to the future
we surrender to rock n roll
we surrender to nobody at all.
We surrender to the new storm that forms in hearts of children.
We will pay the price for they become.

2

Its time to make a deal with the roaches,
the new landlords of the SROs
sooner or later they will demand their own churches be built on the grave of
La Guardia.

Everything we borrow from time vanishes with its vegetable decay
the cords no longer bend
only snap under heavy fingers like old film.

And the last visions fade
with nothing left to say.

Part 2

Exit Zero

We were somewhere in the Blue Ridge Mountains, driving far too fast for these parts with an eighth of pot in the glove compartment. We had rented a piece of shit 1985 Ford that was due at the rental office in Columbia, South Carolina in less than 10 hours. The radio was blasting notes throughout the forest, "Five to one baby, one and five, no one here gets out of here alive now."

In the South, the senses run overtime, you can feel something sinister in the air but you can't put your finger on it. There is something foul in the heart of America. There is nothing permanent here, transient cities, living museums and voodoo angels, ghosts of slaves and surfs with their spells that alter the cleft of the mind. Plantations, ghosts of the South, horrid imprints in time. The laughter of Lucifer reverberates in the minds of the French quarters.

My brother and I were returning from New York to South Carolina. A transient move as it turns out. The old gold miner saying: "Go west young man and seek your fame fortune." And we did. We had been smoking weed and taking the last of our mushrooms since we left New York. There was the sense of the usual paranoia in the car but, we contributed that to prolonged smoking. It was internal and despite the waves of hallucinogenic sensations we knew the fear was living inside like a ravenous tapeworm with no sense of satisfaction, there was nothing on the horizon we were overly concerned about.

Nothing could have prepared us for was what was around the corner. There was no indication of negative vibrations in the air, the monkey hides under the eyelid when danger is on the horizon. So it took us by surprise when the lights behind us started flashing red and blue. "Oh shit," muttered my brother. "I can't believe this." Cops here are home grown like insane plants of the confederacy, Dixie boys with shit-kicker grins. They hang you in these parts. He (my brother) pulled over to the side of the road with twisted anger that was well known to those around him. It was at this time we realized that it was a parks ranger of law enforcement. (Quick note: in some parts of the county, park rangers have the authority of a police officer until a real cop appears on the scene. This is a dangerous practice of course when one considers the difference in training in keeping control of a situation.)

Out of the patrol car we watched him stroll to the driver's side of the car. He walked with a farm-boy's stride, a real apron-monkey. He was young, 22, perhaps, maybe even younger. He had all the makings of a local; fiery red hair, small town stare of someone who was sure they will be home for dinner, no knife fights on his route, farm boy simplicity, never learned how to mistrust or lose well, and was pale as moonlight. At first things seemed to go smoothly, no signs of bad energy or potentially volatile situations. "Can I see your Id and registration please," he asked with an all-too-friendly persona. "You know why I pulled you over?"…. "You boys were speedin', going seventy-five. We have to be careful with the critters around here." My brother stared straight ahead while trying to explain his way of this situation. "I'm sorry but, I lost track of how fast I was going. We just need to get home before tomorrow, you understand."

The park ranger stared at him for a second. My brother's hair was a little past his shoulders and uncombed. His face revealed a hippie that was born far too late, unshaven and thin. His clothes were starting to show the signs of being worn for four days straight. My own hair was long, ragged dark brown locks, complete with full beard and moustache. Our friend moved to the passenger side and demanded to see my ID. Luckily I had my old card. I say "luckily" because normally I don't carry any identification on me; a habit that I fell into for no apparent reason. He took our information back to his car. It should be noted at this time that the license plate on our rental car was for a city in Florida, notorious for their gang violence and drug-related crime. The mushrooms were starting to go sideways on us.

Abruptly the scene changed, someone got the films mixed up and spliced the wrong movies together: Mayberry with the horrors of Deliverance. I could see that our friend's face had changed dramatically when he re-appeared, as if he just caught John Dillinger or one of the Manson family. His already pale complexion now seemed devoid of all pigment and his eyes were now the size of half dollars. His hand was shaking, poised on his gun. Now at the drivers side door.

"You boys got *guns*? You boys got *drugs*? You boys got *al*-ka-hol?" he demanded. "You boys got *guns*? You boys got *drugs*? You boys got *al*-ka-hol?"

"*No!*" we both said, now in a full panic. What had gone wrong? Were we fugitives in some FBI sting? The tide had taken a horrid turn and this adult version of Howdy Doody with an attitude was now clearly looking for any reason to slap the cuffs on us. The questioning continued, "You boys got *guns*? You boys got *drugs*? You boys got *al*-ka-hol?"

"You boys got *guns*? You boys got *drugs*? You boys got *al*-ka-hol?"

We continued our frantic denial of possessing any paraphernalia. It was apparent that he had yet to cut his teeth and couldn't get us to confess to his questioning though he was sure that we were guilty of something but, found no reason to pursue what was turning into a chess game. Quick note: Chess like any other competition is contingent on keeping ones opponent guessing.

Finally he walked back to his car. "*Fucker!*" I gasped finally, now sensing that the worst was over. "Calm down," my brother shouted back, "I know how you get. Don't do anything stupid; I'm just glad he didn't search the car." "Why," I asked. Before my question could be answered the ranger had returned.

"You can pay this by mail or appear in court and pay it there. Keep your speed down." He strolled back to his car then was gone. My brother looked at the ticket, "Fucking pig!!! Seventy –five dollars, oh you mother fucker! Oh, what a shit head" And we drove away.

Ten minutes later I broke wall of the silence and twisted anger. "So why were you so scared he was going to search the car? What was it, the pot?"

"That too" he said, "But I have a sheet of acid in the binder on the back seat."

Night fell when we finally descended from the mountains, reaching the lonely and sorrowful Southern highway, past ghost towns, burned-out farms, fierce churches that permeate the mindless rants of insane preachers of hair-shirt rage; corn-fed children of rickets with crustacean's eyes, their mothers with sinister, poisonous stares standing among chicken shit, coal chalk smeared across their foreheads and arms and invisible eyes that watch among the trees, guardians of the south who make sure you only pass by and keep on movin'.

www.ingramcontent.com/pod-product-compliance
Lightning Source LLC
Chambersburg PA
CBHW031422040426
42444CB00005B/676